WALES

THE FIRST PLACE

WALES

THE FIRST PLACE

JAN MORRIS & PAUL WAKEFIELD

BARNES
&NOBLE
BOOKS
NEW YORK

**This edition published by Barnes & Noble, Inc.
by arrangement with Brockhampton Press Ltd.**

**1998 Barnes & Noble
ISBN 0-7607-0947-5
M 10 9 8 7 6 5 4 3 2 1**

Text © 1982 by Jan Morris
Photographs © 1982 by Paul Wakefield
Poems translated by Twm Morys and Jan Morris

The poem 'Yr Heniaith' from *Dail Pren* by Waldo Williams is reproduced by permission of Gomer Press, Llandysul, Dyfed, Wales.

Previous page TWMPA, BLACK MOUNTAINS, POWYS JANUARY

Printed at Oriental Press, Dubai, U.A.E.

STAYING AND GOING

The mighty mountains changeless stand,
    Tireless the winds across them blow;
The shepherds' song across the land
    Sounds with the dawn as long ago.
Still around the rocks each day
    The bright white daisies nod and climb.
Only the shepherds cannot stay
    Upon those hills till end of time.

Old Welsh customs need must change
    As years progress from age to age.
The generations each arrange
    Their own brief patterns on the page.
After his long watch on the hill
    Alun Mabon too has gone.
Yet lives the ancient language still,
    And still the melodies play on.

JOHN CEIRIOG HUGHES (1832-87)

trans. Jan Morris

The first place? On paper, as in vulgar reputation, Wales more often seems one of the last. A protrusion on the western edge of England is all it appears on the map, a bump upon the European perimeter: half barren, half empty, in which two and a half million people, a fifth of them speaking a language that nobody else understands, scratch, scrape, dig or wheedle an often unstable living from a mostly ungenerous environment – far from the sources of power or entertainment, where the drizzle mercilessly falls, where sheep get trapped in the high winter snowdrifts, where pubs are liable to close on Sundays, where roads meander agonizingly around bare mountain massifs, where mines foul the southern valleys and trailer camps the northern shores, where industry seems to lurch perpetually from recession to redundancy, and a long emigration of disheartened country-men leaves a hundred thousand homesteads open to the stars, or prettied up as holiday homes by an alien bourgeoisie in order to be burnt to the ground by nationalist zealots.

There are times, I confess, especially when the weather is grey, when I look out of my own Welsh window and am tempted to feel, just for a moment, that these despondent stereotypes represent the truth. The Celtic Sea lies empty out there, all traffic gone, the sheep nibble monotonously in the meadow, the mountains are half hidden in rain-cloud, and a hangdog resignation seems to extend across the country, as though it is suspended for ever between events. Presently, though, almost always, that twinge of despair is succeeded by another emotion altogether, something more akin to the visionary, or perhaps the possessed. I am Anglo-Welsh, Welsh father, English mother. On one level of my consciousness I do sometimes share the impatient hopelessness habitually inspired in the English by the prospect of Wales: but on a deeper level my patrimony exerts itself, and as I lean from my window in the stillness I feel stirring within me a sensation which is partly love, and partly pity, and partly pride, but largely a kind of insatiable dream, a never-to-be-fulfilled conviction that out there somewhere another country is concealed, another time lurks, and some hidden key to the understanding of things is waiting to be turned.

There is no English word for this queer insight, but the Welsh word *hiraeth*, though long ago sentimentalized in translation as a sort of maudlin homesickness, does partly explain it. It means a longing, but especially a longing for something indefinable, perhaps unattainable: a longing for beginnings maybe, or for conclusions, or perhaps, in the Welsh idiom that Shakespeare satirized as 'skimble-skamble stuff', for some sort of ill-defined and hazily conceived reconciliation. It is a yearning, you might say, for primacies: and it is because of this instinctive affinity with original or ultimate matters, the very antithesis of the fashionable or the provincial, that I venture to call Wales 'The First Place'.

Ours is a country that reveals itself only in layers, and sometimes only to the inner eye, but in those skimble-skamble moments I see exemplified in it the Four Elements themselves, the foundation of all things: the earth rich in the old loyalties of the place – the water flowing so fresh through its poetry, so evasive through its doubts – the fire flaming in its unsuspected passions – the air drifting tantalizingly, full of allusion, past my open window in the morning, or through the silent images of this book.

DAEAR : EARTH

Wales as a substance, so to speak, is immensely old. It seems to have been there always. Other countries may have older structures, but only just – the oldest Welsh monuments are thought to be as old as the pyramids. None have older rocks, the Cambrian mountains being, so geologists say, as old as any on earth. Not many populations can claim a more deeply rooted pedigree: the Celts who form the core of it have been living in this small corner of the world for several thousand years. No country in the Western world has an older language or literature: the Welsh language, still spoken by half a million people, has been in continuous literary use since the sixth century at least. Nor can many nations claim a more resilient sense of identity, for though Wales has seldom been a single independent country, its peculiar style and self-awareness have survived conquests by Romans and Normans, savagings by Irish, Vikings and Saxons, and seven centuries of English domination, so that today its 8,000 square miles are recognizable still as a land separate and different from any other.

AFON TWYMYN, CAMBRIAN MOUNTAINS, POWYS   JULY

AFON LLEDR, BETWS-Y-COED, GWYNEDD   JANUARY

Wales has always thought itself a special place. Alone among all the territories of the western Roman Empire it was never over-run by the barbarians, and through all its later tumults its people held in trust, as it were, not only the civilizing achievements of the Romans, but Christianity too, and beliefs and ideas far older still – the dimly remembered cultures of the Druids and the Celtic animists, and of those Other People, whoever they were, who built the megaliths. All was transmuted, the Christian, the Roman, the Celtic, the arcane prehistoric, into myth and tradition: and so through it all the personality of Wales itself, expressed in language, in landscape, in atmosphere and in the nature of society, remained obdurately itself.

Although since 1536 Wales has been absorbed into the United Kingdom of Great Britain, the nature of this country, in fact as in symbolism, remains stubbornly resilient still. Consider the Rhondda Fawr Valley, the most famous of the coal valleys of South Wales, celebrated in novel, movie, legend and sentimental memoir. It is said to be one of the most thickly populated places in Europe, and all along its narrow cleft beside the river the Victorian terrace houses are jam-packed cheek-by-jowl, far down the valley from Blaencwm to Pontypridd – one long urban zone, one community running into another, one chapel succeeding (or disputing) the next. It looks more like a geological than a human process, a glacial flow of buildings, a masonry drift, mile after mile from the mountains to the sea.

But if you climb the hill called Penrhys, high above Tonypandy in the very heart of Rhondda, you will discover that process in reverse. Slowly, almost imperceptibly, the earth is reclaiming its own. Where once those blackened settlements crawled year by year ever higher up the mountain slopes, now the green is coming back, in patches, and strips, in mere hints or possibilities of green, wherever the eye falls. As the coal mines are progressively worked out, as their huge black slag-heaps are reclaimed or overgrown and the smoke of their engines disappears, so, gently but inexorably, the old balance is restored once more, and Wales reverts to its origins.

In this country the earth usually wins. Even in the heyday of Welsh coal and iron, when these valleys were prodigies of energy, profit, exploitation, dirt, talent, congestion, fellowship and politics – even then Rhondda and its neighbour-valleys never did obliterate the mountains all around, which held themselves aloof through it all, pristine with grass and bracken above the smoke-filled towns below. All over Wales, down the centuries, industries have come and gone: lead and gold mines, from Roman times to the nineteenth century, the slate and copper industries of the north, quarries of many kinds, mineral works, textile mills – most of them extinct now, leaving behind only grassy mounds, ruined cottages, unexplained tunnels in the hills, museums and tourist revivals. It is as though this ancient organism, tolerating an alien graft for a generation or two, rejects it in the end, and returns to its own metabolism.

The interior of Wales is high and difficult country, from the magnificent peaks of Eryri, Snowdonia, in the north, down through the bare uplands of mid-Wales to the Brecon Beacon mountain range of the south. Around

AFON MELLTE, YSTRADFELLTE, POWYS   OCTOBER

AFON RHEIDOL, DEVIL'S BRIDGE, DYFED   MARCH

LLYN Y FAN FAWR, BLACK MOUNTAIN, POWYS   MARCH

CROMLECH, DYFFRYN ARDUDWY, GWYNEDD   MARCH

and through these highlands fertile plains and river valleys flourish, but generally speaking Welsh soil is thin, Welsh gradients are demanding, and the generic Welshman survives now, as he always did, only when he is on the right terms with the earth itself, its textures and its undulations. This is a stone country, hard and jagged, and the most lasting of the human artifacts raised upon it are those that assimilate most closely to its own forms.

The oldest of them all, the standing stones and megalithic circles which are to be found in almost every corner of Wales, suit the earth so perfectly that they sometimes seem an actual part of it; it is only when the pattern of their construction emerges, when you realize one lonely stone to be aligned upon another, or a pile of boulders to be more than a random heap, that they are seen to be human works at all. The dry-stone walls of Wales, half-toppled often, or lichen-clad on their long march across the mountains, are themselves like contour lines. The Welsh upland farms, long and low among their outhouses, seem to have occupied their sites so long that they have gone beyond mere architecture: they have adapted to their settings organically over the generations, an extra cow-house in one century, a new porch in another, layer after layer of whitewash on the walls, long-patched roofs of slate, tile or corrugated iron, and in the course of it all they seem actually to have joined themselves to the rocks beneath their floors, and become outcrops themselves.

They are mostly isolated buildings. The Celts were people of centrifugal instinct, and it was the Normans who introduced the idea of the town to this country. Even now the market towns established by the

CAPEL DEWI, DYFED   APRIL

NEAR ABERGORLECH, DYFED   APRIL

conquering English in the Middle Ages look slightly uneasy in their environment: rather too calculated somehow, with their ordered streets and their dominant church towers, their squirely mansion on the outskirts, their disciplined housing estates and their big glass-walled schools. To this day they do not altogether fit, and if you are in Llanidloes, say, or Llandovery on market day, when the sheep-farmers and the cattle-men throng the streets and jam the pubs, you may sometimes have the curious feeling that these men are visitors from some other society altogether, only waiting for the last sale to vanish once more to their own inaccessible terrains.

A strong strain of animism, the belief that God resides in all natural things, even in rocks and running water, has infused Welsh thought since the earliest times. Welsh poets have habitually approached nature in a distinctively robust and direct way, treating the other creatures in particular as if they were equals, sometimes amenable, sometimes curmudgeonly. The beasts are not scorned, patronized or sentimentalized. They are messengers or conspirators, they are asked for advice, they hoot too loud at night. They are often satirized and sometimes anathematized. Like the sun and the stars, which played so compelling a part in the lives of the first inhabitants of Wales, the birds, beasts, fish and insects are part of the grand community, essential to the pattern that contains night and day, hill and valley, land and sea, man and woman and God himself.

This old familiarity with the animals is still apparent everywhere in Wales, where there are more sheep than there are humans. Even in the dense industrial valleys sheep casually wander, nibbling garden roses and

DR CULE WITH TWIN WELSH COBS SIAN AND SIONED, PENCADER, DYFED   APRIL

MR REISS WITH WELSH MOUNTAIN PONY, LLANYBYDDER, DYFED   APRIL

being sworn at by maddened householders, and country roads are often blocked by woolly seas of them, barked about by frantic dogs and prodded along by shepherds. The partnership of the Welsh farmer and his dog is generally affectionate but sometimes distinctly caustic, just like the relationship between the medieval bards and their owls, foxes and seagulls, and on the high moorlands you may still see farmers riding their mountain ponies with the same sort of throwaway comradeship.

To see the Welshman's association with the animals at its most compelling, try going to the monthly horse fair at Llanybydder in Dyfed, said to be the largest in Europe: for there, so long have man and horse been working together, so delusive is the strange alliance, that it is sometimes hard to tell which is master, which is servant. Cob and farmer, girl and mountain pony, parade apparently as equals through the sales ring, or wander side by side through the yard outside: and when the boys come clopping helter-skelter down the village street, waving their sticks and shouting as they career between the market-stalls, they seem gloriously united with their horses in exuberant cahoots.

Today half the Welsh people live in the industrial towns and cities of the perimeter – Cardiff the capital, Swansea, Newport, Merthyr Tydfil, Wrexham and the rest. Here as everywhere cosmopolitan modernism, along with television, the family car, the tractor and the washing machine, has changed the feel of things during the past half century. Still however this must remain one of the earthiest of Western countries. It is not simply the continuing wildness of so much of the terrain, it is a human instinct

VALE OF EWYAS, BLACK MOUNTAINS, POWYS   JANUARY

too, passed down the generations of Welshness. When the summer floods rise on my own river at home, and the sea-trout begin their majestic night run out of the sea into the mountain lakes above, I know that now as ever down on the river bank, in the dark of the shrubbery, the wink of a torch, the smell of home-rolled cigarettes, will betray the presence of the village fishermen, drawn like migrants themselves intuitively to that green rushing darkness. Today, as always, the men of the mining towns take their whippets to the high mountain ridges on Sunday mornings, and the coracle men of Teifi and Tywi launch their immemorial craft, unchanged for a thousand years, upon the evening tide. There can be few more authentic folk-figures, straight from the Middle Ages, than the young Welsh trapper, still to be seen in the Black Mountains or in the Preseli lanes, swaggering home from his traps in gumboots and raggety shirt, with a couple of red foxes slung over his shoulder. And who could be more truly rooted in his own geology than the thick-set, short-legged Welsh farmer, born very likely of fifty generations on the same soil, when he stoops to pick up a great stone from the ditch, and with a gentle flexing of his muscles, a slow tightening of his back, a bit of a grunt, lifts its great mass gently from the ground as he might lift a living creature from its resting-place.

It is only proper that the traditional industries of Wales have mostly been industries of the earth. The coal industry in particular, in its titanic style and meaning, brutally honoured the nature of the country, and in the days when millions of tons of coal were extracted from the southern valleys every year, when the ships in their thousands sailed from the Welsh coal

ports for the markets of the world, when 25,000 people lived in every square mile of the Rhondda, its passions, like its profits and its sufferings, were always very close to the ground.

In those days the tall black scaffold that housed the pit-wheel, looming over almost every valley community, became itself a kind of totem, a direct successor to the great megaliths by which, several millennia before, the people of this same landscape had proclaimed their affinity with the rocks beneath. The pit-wheel dominated everything, sometimes still and silent, sometimes spinning and whirring: each morning the miners set off at its command like pilgrims to a shrine, and like so many sacrifices the pit-wheel sent them, crammed in their iron cages, plummeting into the depths of Wales.

DŴR : WATER

If the images of Wales are often monolithic, they are often liquid too. This is a country surrounded on three sides by the sea, and watered everywhere by magnificent lakes and rivers, black, secret and allegedly bottomless in high mountain hollows, pouring in their hundreds over cataracts and through rocky defiles from the uplands to the coasts. Water is a very Welsh element. It was out of the sea that the Welsh saints came: the wandering holy men who, perilously navigating the Irish Sea in their leather coracles, settled on capes and islands all around the shores of Wales, establishing their lonely hermitages, building simple churches, performing miracles, and leaving behind them a particular limpidity that has never quite been obscured.

The greatest of them all, Dewi Sant, the patron saint of Wales, is commemorated in the cathedral of St David's near the coast of Dyfed. The village that attends it is an austere little place, wind-huddled, flat on the ground, almost treeless, and the cathedral itself has an embattled air too, sunk as it is in a deep rocky hollow as protection against climate and sea-raiders alike. Inside the building, though, a special sort of watery light

LAKE VYRNWY, POWYS   AUGUST

SGŴD ISAF CLUN-GWYN, AFON MELLTE, YSTRADFELLTE, POWYS   NOVEMBER

is dominant: more than just a light indeed, a greyish, bluish quality of being, emanating partly from the sandstone of the building, but much more I think from the nature of the place – holy for so long, so close to the sea and the rocks, so impregnated with the oldest memories of life along these shores, and having at its very heart, behind the high altar, the bones of Dewi Sant himself, which seem to generate from behind their iron grille, out of their richly enamelled casket, some pool-like refulgence of their own.

This limpid liquidity finds its perfect instrument in the Welsh language, which is the very opposite of the four-square, hard-cornered Latinate languages, and indeed is so fond of slur and elision that its initial letters often mutate, to facilitate the glide from one word to the next – a process aptly called in Welsh *treiglad*, wandering. The language proclaims its mellifluous and idiosyncratic meander for all to see in its place names: Llanrhaeadr-ym-Mochnant (The Holy Place by the Falls of the Pig's Brook), Moel Llys-y-Coed (The Bare Mountain of the Court of the Wood), or Pistyll Rhaeadr, which simply means, in a robustly indigenous form of emphasis, Waterfall Cataract.

Once such sounds were heard over much of Europe, in the days when the Celts were powerful from Turkey to Ireland, but gradually conquerors' tongues replaced them, until today the Celtic languages are spoken only in Ireland, in the western parts of Scotland, vestigially in Cornwall, in Brittany and in Wales: and of these survivors only Welsh can presently claim to be a complete contemporary tongue, spoken by many

LLŶN PENINSULA, GWYNEDD   OCTOBER

IRFON, POWYS   JUNE

people as their ordinary vernacular, but expressing itself also in the full range of poetry, novels, magazines, plays, television shows, rock lyrics, satirical reviews and official documents.

It is in the Welsh language that the 'otherness' of Wales most obviously resides: for though anyone can hear it spoken in Wales, and see its symptoms all around in road signs and bilingual pamphlets, the culture that attends it, the frame of mind, the manner of thought, is all but impenetrable to those who do not understand it. The Welsh-speaking Welsh, the Cymry Cymraeg, form an inner people within the nation, exciting often the scorn or irritation of the English-speaking majority, but more usually I think the envy. The private nature of the tongue, its legendary pithiness and precision, its vast wealth of idioms and proverbial sayings – all this gives it a strange allure, intoxicating to those who know it, infuriating to the rest.

Welsh is a life-giving language. It makes the Cymry Cymraeg, often diffident and defensive when they are speaking English, superbly confident when they break into Welsh, releasing all their wit and speed of response: as Giraldus Cambrensis remarked as long ago as the twelfth century, 'these people being of a sharp and acute intellect ... are more quick and cunning than the other inhabitants of a western clime'. In parts of Wales where the language has died one often feels a melancholy emptiness in the air, something missing, something saddened: conversely in parts where it is still vigorously alive its presence provides an ancient solace and stimulation, sealing friendships, maintaining loyalties, and making everything seem more virile and vivacious.

English people often live in Wales for years without mastering a syllable of this magnificent language, even when it is spoken all around them; but this is not entirely their own fault. Welsh has survived at all partly on account of its deliberate separateness, which has enabled it to evade rather than resist the pressures of its mighty neighbour, English; and the Welsh-speaking minority of Wales, like the *tylwyth teg* or Fair People of the old Welsh tales, lives a double life. There is a legend of North Wales which tells of a respectable householder who is accused by the *tylwyth teg* of throwing his slops down the chimneys of their houses – their subterranean town being situated, all unknown to him, immediately below his own front doorstep. So it is often enough with the world of the Cymry Cymraeg, which is always there, but not always to be seen. The insensitive settler in Wales can spend half a lifetime without knowing what is happening all around him – his next-door neighbour may be a celebrity within the Welsh culture and he will never know it, the polite young student home from college may well be, for all the outsider can tell, one of those wild nationalist zealots he reads about in the newspapers.

So a stranger can seldom quite put a finger on this indestructible wraith of Welshness. It is like quicksilver all around him: or like water, glinting sometimes in a sudden shaft of sunlight, but often lying unnoticeable, deep and still, up among the mountain ridges.

If the watery element symbolizes something hard to pin down in Wales, it symbolizes too a restlessness often apparent in the people. Whether or not they speak the language, the Welsh are generally devoted to their own

FLIMSTON BAY, DYFED   DECEMBER

NEWBOROUGH WARREN, ANGLESEY   SEPTEMBER

particular patch of country, to farm or valley, Cardiff pub or chapel in Llanrhaeadr-ym-Mochnant. But they have often been a wandering people too, as though from time to time they have felt the need to break away from these old grey walls and changeless mountains. They have gone off in search of jobs of course, but also in search of wider, less material prospects, and they have come home again, as often as not, rich in experience as in hard cash. This makes for an ironic dichotomy in the spirit of Wales. While Welsh people who stay at home can be more than usually stay-at-home, Welshmen who have travelled seem gifted with an extra dimension of freedom, as though they have been permanently liberated from the smallness and oldness of Wales itself, and carry around with them, wherever they are, some serendipitous advantage of release.

Often, when they themselves are dead and gone, this exhilarating spirit of enlargement seems to linger around their absence, like a ghost of old excitements. I feel it sometimes on the drovers' roads, the rough tracks which, striking across the high moorlands of central Wales, once took the great herds of black Welsh cattle to their English markets. These were indeed routes to emancipation for the drovers, who became among the best-informed men in Wales as a result of their journeys. Even now I like to fancy I hear their bold cries in those lonely places, '*Haiptrw Ho! Haip, haip, haiptrw Ho!*', and smell the sweat and leather of their passing, and feel their pace quicken – horses, men, dogs and cattle alike – as they see the pine trees, far away below the escarpment, which tell them that a tavern is near, one stage more in the high road to the great world outside...

GLASLYN AND LLIWEDD, SNOWDONIA, GWYNEDD   MAY

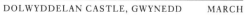

DOLWYDDELAN CASTLE, GWYNEDD   MARCH

particular patch of country, to farm or valley, Cardiff pub or chapel in Llanrhaeadr-ym-Mochnant. But they have often been a wandering people too, as though from time to time they have felt the need to break away from these old grey walls and changeless mountains. They have gone off in search of jobs of course, but also in search of wider, less material prospects, and they have come home again, as often as not, rich in experience as in hard cash. This makes for an ironic dichotomy in the spirit of Wales. While Welsh people who stay at home can be more than usually stay-at-home, Welshmen who have travelled seem gifted with an extra dimension of freedom, as though they have been permanently liberated from the smallness and oldness of Wales itself, and carry around with them, wherever they are, some serendipitous advantage of release.

Often, when they themselves are dead and gone, this exhilarating spirit of enlargement seems to linger around their absence, like a ghost of old excitements. I feel it sometimes on the drovers' roads, the rough tracks which, striking across the high moorlands of central Wales, once took the great herds of black Welsh cattle to their English markets. These were indeed routes to emancipation for the drovers, who became among the best-informed men in Wales as a result of their journeys. Even now I like to fancy I hear their bold cries in those lonely places, '*Haiptrw Ho! Haip, haip, haiptrw Ho!*', and smell the sweat and leather of their passing, and feel their pace quicken – horses, men, dogs and cattle alike – as they see the pine trees, far away below the escarpment, which tell them that a tavern is near, one stage more in the high road to the great world outside...

More ironically, I sometimes detect a similar fructifying sense of opportunity in the mansions of those Welsh squires of the eighteenth and nineteenth centuries who, educated or indoctrinated in England, chose to live in the English way upon their Welsh estates. Some of them were sots and bullies, lording it over their backwood kingdoms with a squalid arrogance, but others brought home to their often poverty-stricken properties some vital radical energy from outside. The best of them tried to unite the graces of the wider world with the wild grandeur of Wales, and so gave their own specific meaning to the concept of the Picturesque – their houses illuminated with Gothick fantasies and packed with books and sculptures from the Grand Tour, their hospitality wonderfully urbane and up-to-date, but all around them still, inescapable for all their Improvements, the bogs, crags and silences of rural Wales, and the language they had forgotten or foresworn.

And most pervasively of all, naturally, a sense of release still permeates the seaports of Wales. Until the coming of the railways almost everything that was new, for good or for evil, entered this country through its ports, whether it was by ferry over the Bristol Channel, by coracle over the Irish Sea, or by schooner or tall ship from the Americas or Australia. In a country so dense of texture, so stacked with mountains, with such awful roads, the ports were like open windows, and their influences ran away up the valleys behind them: the influence of the saintly hermits, through the little havens of the west; the influence of Norman barons and English industrialists, up the valleys of the south; the influence of Lancashire holiday-makers, along the piers of the north coast; the

LLANGRANNOG, DYFED   JANUARY

DOLWYDDELAN CASTLE, GWYNEDD   MARCH

AFON FFYNNON-DDEWI, DYFED   JUNE

influence of the Irish around the ferry ports of Fishguard and Holyhead; the influence of all the world through the deep-sea ports of Gwynedd, in the far north-west – which even now, when the ocean traffic has long since died and the harbours have been handed over to yachtsmen and inshore fishing-boats, give to that part of Wales a special openness and freedom.

Up there the old slate port of Porthmadog, above all others, pungently evokes the Welsh sense of wander and curiosity, coupled always with a compelling love of home. It is many a long year since the last of the Porthmadog deep-sea ships put to sea, but the town is still full of their memories and effects: not just in the snug stone-walled harbour, now filled with yachts and dinghies, but in the very aspect and manner of the place – its old seamen's pubs (The Ship, The Australia), its handsome terraced captains' houses, its seamanlike posture, so to speak, looking away from the mountain mass of Eryri over the sand-bar to the open sea.

At the turn of our century the whole life of Porthmadog was geared to the sea. The schooners that were built here, the celebrated Western Ocean Yachts, were among the finest sailing-vessels ever made. Their crews, Welsh-speaking local men almost to a hand, took them on immense voyages across the Atlantic, into the Baltic and the Mediterranean, down the East African coast. Their owners were truly the people of Porthmadog: blacksmiths, tailors, carpenters, clergymen and many housewives were all capitalists in this communal enterprise. This was the water-element of Wales at its most creative and invigorating, bolstering the assurance and broadening the vision of the people – who flourished grandly about their harbour for a generation or two, until the slate industry collapsed, the last of the Ocean Yachts went to the breakers, and the hills closed in again.

Another kind of Welsh fluidity is part of the country's fascination indeed, but also part of its debilitation. The artistic tradition of the Celts was averse to squares and parallels, revealing itself rather in convolutions of interlocking circles, squiggles and illusory knots, and some of this fondness for elusive complexity survives in the contemporary Welsh manner of thought. It was an American who said that while a Frenchman's truth was akin to a straight line, a Welshman's truth was more in the nature of a curve, and it is a fact that Welsh affairs are entangled always in parabola, double-meaning and implication. This makes for a web-like interest, but it also implies a lack of frankness, and means that the Welsh nation is never quite in step with itself, let alone with anyone else.

You can feel this instability in almost any properly Welsh conversation. It expresses itself less in open disagreement than in a tone of voice, an implied reservation, a change of subject or an emollient suggestion of alternatives – 'Yes, yes, I agree with you of course, you're perfectly right about that, but I do just wonder now, if...?' The Celts were traditionally a people without a nation, an *idea* of a people, and the same shifting and scattered concept of identity affects not only chapel meetings or family conferences, but also the greatest processes of Welsh faith or history.

The Welsh are never as one – except only, perhaps, in their general conviction of Welshness, and even that takes many forms. In the past they were habitually divided into several usually antagonistic kingdoms; more

SEA FROM LLANGELYNNIN, GWYNEDD   FEBRUARY

AFON LLOER, SNOWDONIA, GWYNEDD   FEBRUARY

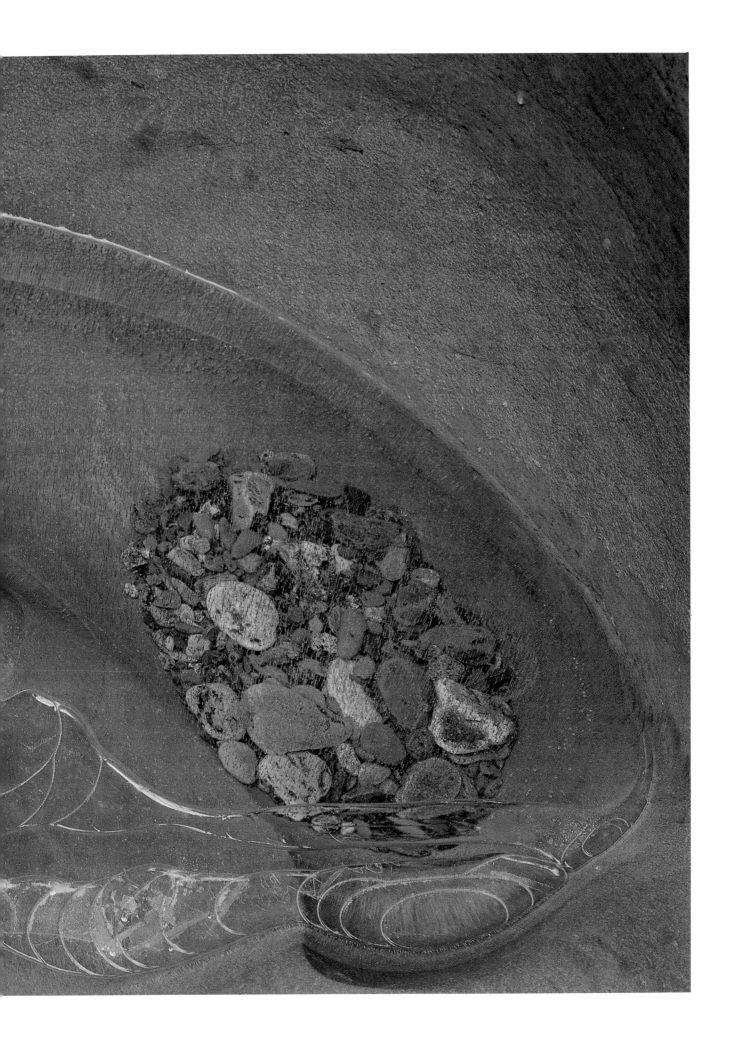

AFON NEDD, YSTRADFELLTE, POWYS   OCTOBER

AFON TYWI, DINAS, DYFED   MAY

recently they have been split into mutually antagonistic Christian sects. Some Welshmen have always been friends of England, some have always been her enemies. Some have been resolutely cosmopolitan, some fiercely isolationist. In our own time North is endemically suspicious of South, and vice versa, while Welsh-speakers look down on English-speakers, English-speakers resent the pretensions of Welsh-speakers, separatists fight against loyalists, romantic interpreters of Welsh history battle with stern dialectical determinists. Nothing is ever settled in Wales. It is a country in flow, always on an ebbing or a rising tide, never actually at the turn.

As a result there hang over this superb countryside, over this talented and distinctive people, several vague but enervating torments, less like thunderclouds than like those drifting cumulae which, even on the finest Welsh summer days, are apt to cast you into shadow now and then. You might call them, in the tradition of the Welsh mystic triads, the Three Torments of Wales. There is the Torment of the Torn Tongue – the curse of a society ripped apart by its own language. There is the Torment of the Confused Loyalty – to Welshness or to Britishness, to country or to Crown? There is the Torment of Disunity, that old, old conflict down the ages, region against region, interest against interest, creed against creed.

There is a fourth torment, too: the Torment of the Grey Day, the one I mentioned at the start of this essay. This is the troubled sense which so often overcomes the Welsh patriot, the feeling that these myriad waters, leaping and tumbling out of the soul of Wales, diverted here, bog-consumed there, will never run obligingly, as other waters do, peaceful and smiling to the sea.

LLYN LOGIN, MYNYDD EPPYNT, POWYS   JULY

TÂN : FIRE

The story of Wales is one of bitter defiance, a fight that can never be won, but is never quite lost either. Seven hundred years after the final conquest of Wales by Edward I of England, the patriots continue the battle to save their language and their national identity – fighting these days against apathy and sometimes hostility in their own country, lack of understanding in England, and the vast pressure towards conformity and materialism in the Western world at large.

This is a tragic endowment, but gripping too. Half the enthralment of Wales is in the struggle of it, and its character depends upon its continuing bloody-mindedness. It is a prickly place, a huge concentric fortress of national awareness. Outside the ramparts of course there are plenty of Welshmen who do not want to fight at all, who have been deracinated or untribalized altogether, and who would happily see the nation consumed into the blander whole of Euro-America. Within the ramparts, though, there are successive rings of resistance. The outer ring fights simply for an attitude: these not very formidable defences are manned by comedians,

LLYN DINAS, SNOWDONIA, GWYNEDD   MAY

CWM GWAUN, DYFED   JUNE

professional Welshmen in saloon bars, rugby supporters and all those who believe that being amusingly Welshy of intonation is patriotism enough. The middle ring is manned by people who are ready to be assimilated into the wider world in material and political ways, but who fight for Welshness of a deeper kind – for its particular social relationships, for its music and its literature, for its landscapes. And in the tight-barred keep at the core of it, moated against internal traitors as against enemies from outside, the last-ditch Cymry Cymraeg stand perpetually to their arms – devoted with a passionate zeal to their soil, their history, their nationhood, their language and everything else that is Welsh.

The siege is never over, and wherever you look upon these earthworks warriors are waving spears or banners, shouting slogans, sharpening knives, or lighting torches for the Fire.

Let us visit the Crowning of the Bard at the National Eisteddfod, the annual celebration, or re-dedication, of Welshness at its most Welsh. For many Welsh people this is the supreme moment of the year, the perennial climax of the long resistance. The Eisteddfod is peripatetic in the Celtic tradition, being held in North and South Wales on alternate years. It is the largest folk festival in Europe, and its field really does look, from any nearby vantage point, rather like a military encampment – a huge assembly of tents, pavilions and caravans which in the course of the week becomes, like most fortifications in the front line, a bit muddy underfoot and a bit battered-looking around the sandbags. Its morale never flags though. Every day the immense crowds, drawn from all over Wales, wander and

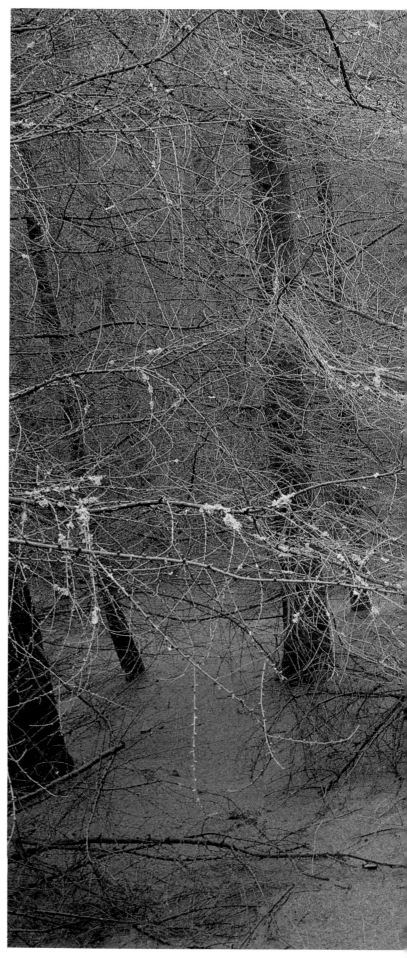

BLAEN-Y-GLYN, BRECON BEACONS, POWYS   MARCH

gossip around the wide central field, and music sounds incessantly over the loudspeakers, and visiting celebrities are snatched for television interviews, and there are poets striding here and there devising extempore verses for literary competitions, and male voice choirs spilling out of buses, and girls carrying harps, and stalls selling Welsh pop records, Dictionaries of Welsh Biography, manifestoes for the Welsh Language Society or the Daughters of the Dawn, patriotic car stickers, wooden figures of coracle men, T-shirts advertising the Welsh Order of Hope, scurrilous political broadsheets and many, many Bibles.

The unmistakable focus of it all is the great pavilion in the centre, said to be the largest portable building in the world, and there on the right day, if we can find ourselves seats in its cavernous interior, we will see the Welsh fire burning at its most theatrical. Assembled on stage are the Bards of the Druidical Order, a strange conclave of eminent citizens, doctors and philosophers, writers and politicians, dressed in long hooded robes of white and grey. They are presided over by ancient sages and attended by nymphs in green, by matrons with horns of plenty, by harpists and by trumpeters, and they are there to crown the winner of the chief poetry contest as Bard and hero of his nation – perhaps the greatest honour that the Cymry Cymraeg have to offer.

The winner's identity is a secret, but he is sitting, we know, somewhere in the audience around us. A hum of excitement and speculation accordingly fills the pavilion. Strange preliminaries occur on stage: harpists pluck weird strains, elves dance, a gigantic sword is half-drawn from its sheath, then majestically slammed home again. '*Oes*

Heddwch?' cries the Archdruid, 'Is there peace?' *'Heddwch!'* thunders back the audience, and the trumpeters blow their fanfares, and gathering their robes about them the chief Druids gravely leave the stage to summon the victorious poet to his honours. The organ thunders. A spotlight plays at random over the auditorium. The television cameras are poised in their gantries. The audience strains forward. Presently the light steadies itself, sweeps deliberately along the seats, and falls at last upon the person of the winner – who, blushing with pride and self-consciousness, and pretending hard to be astonished, allows himself with mock reluctance to be led away by the Druids, up through that huge applauding crowd, up through the reverberating organ music, to the throne that is, for those few moments, the very crucible of Wales. There nymphs and matrons welcome him, those robed and hooded worthies greet him to their company, and the spiky gold crown of the National Eisteddfod of Wales, made specially for his honour, is placed gently upon his brow.

It is showy, it is a little sentimental, some people find it, with its invented antiquities of ritual and costume, rather silly; but it is unmistakably afire. This passionate and sometimes voluptuous enthusiasm is what the Welsh call *hwyl*. It comes in fits and starts, but its force can be terrific. The average Welsh street-crowd does not look particularly passionate, and the manners of the Welsh are essentially kind and easy-going. Yet all through history the Welsh have been intermittently seized, like the crowd in the Eisteddfod pavilion, by spasms of extraordinary fervour, releasing itself sometimes in fantasy, sometimes in violence, sometimes in art and often in religion.

GORS LWYD, CAMBRIAN MOUNTAINS, DYFED   OCTOBER

Hwyl doubtless fired the Welsh soldiers throughout their centuries of battle against the Saxons, the Normans and the English, and incited those Welsh women who, after particularly satisfactory victories, took to the field to mutilate the enemy dead. *Hwyl* certainly inspired the evangelical preachers of the eighteenth and nineteenth centuries whose mystical spell over their congregations changed the destinies of this country – passionate men themselves, full of fire and force, who brought their sermons to life with tricks of showmanship and splendid flights of rhetoric, and sent their listeners home from chapel desperate with remorse or elated by the certainty of redemption. *Hwyl* sustains the brilliant Welsh rugby teams now, and sustains their supporters too, whose full-throated voicing of Welsh songs in the great national arena of Cardiff Arms Park, especially when the old antagonist England is the visiting team, is very like the roar of the multitude at an older amphitheatre, demanding in particular the abasement of the Lion.

In bad times it is *hwyl* that has saved the Welsh from despair. Even in the heart-breaking days of depression visitors to industrial Wales marvelled at the persistent fun of this people, their wryness and sly humour, their frequent self-mockery. 'I was there!' cries the comedian Max Boyce, the voice of the valleys in the 1980s, and into the catch-phrase is packed a wonderful richness of emotion and experience, braggadocio laced with self-amusement and softened by a touch of true *hiraeth*. If you wave to a passer-by in any Welsh town, ten to one he will wave back: partly out of plain politeness, partly because he thinks he may know you, or because you might be somebody he *ought* to know, like the bank manager or a television personality, but largely because of the man's natural buoyancy and desire to please, which makes him wave rather than not wave, laugh rather than keep a straight face, weep rather than stiffen the upper lip.

For though the Wales of the stereotypes is notorious for dismal Sundays and puritanical taboos, really this country has always been full of merriment. Medieval visitors thought it one of the jolliest countries in Europe, alive with dance, sport and music, and its folk-lore is rich in lusty anecdote and horseplay. Strong drink (to name just one indulgence) has been at once the delight and the bane of the Welsh: one of the earliest known poems in the Welsh language describes a group of Welsh warriors staggering out to war all too well primed with mead, and the princes and lords of independent Wales were proud of their private breweries and imported wines. Under the influence of the Methodist revival the old appetite was distinctly tempered, but today the process is being reversed once more: though parts of Wales are still dry on Sundays, Welshmen are known again for their high-spirited drinking habits, and when the big London brewers want to give the ultimate cachet to a new beer, often enough they use a malt-modulated Welsh voice to advertise it on television.

The Welsh have always been lusty in love, too. Dafydd ap Gwilym, the divine fourteenth-century Welsh poet, wrote about making eyes at the local girls during a Sunday sermon, and in another poem he urges a nun to leave her all and come into the woods with him. When the Commissioners of Inquiry into the State of Education in Wales came in 1847 to the rural

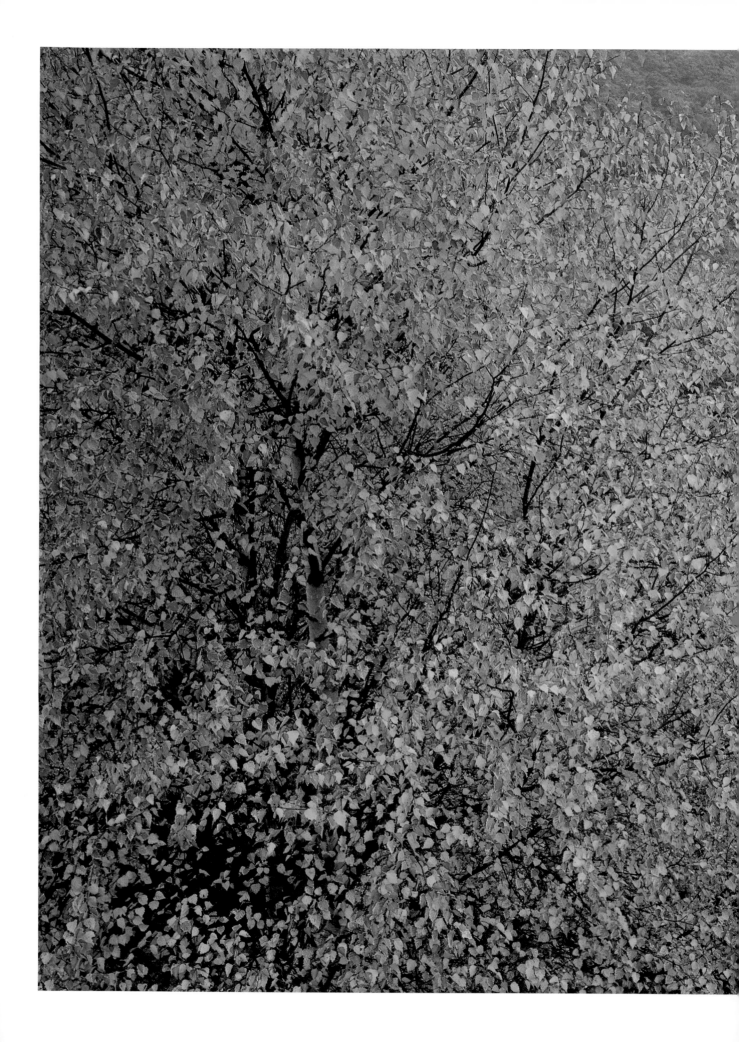

AFON TYWI, DYFED   OCTOBER

areas of the north, they reported that one vice above all others, 'unchecked by any instruments of civilization', was prevalent throughout the region: *Incontinence*, or *Want of Chastity*. Twenty years later, at the height of the evangelical revival, the Dean of St David's found it necessary to insist that the local lifeboat, hitherto kept under covers in the main square of the village, should be removed elsewhere because of the goings-on at night beneath its tarpaulins. By and large the Welsh have retained, even through all the restraints of Calvinism, a tolerant attitude towards this ebullience of the flesh, privately if not publicly: and this is fortunate, because I doubt if there are many Welsh families, rich or poor, church or chapel, whose pedigree does not include one or two Dafydds, Myfanwys, Gareths or Toms born on the wrong side of the blanket.

The virility that makes the Welsh active in pleasure has made them formidable fighting men. If they fought against the English for several centuries, they often fought *for* the English too, in their incessant wars against European rivals and recalcitrant subjects of Empire. Welsh bowmen won the battle of Agincourt against the French in 1415, Welsh riflemen the battle of Rorke's Drift against the Zulus in 1879, and it was a Welsh general who, in the dying days of the British Empire, tried to keep the warring factions from each other's throats during the partitioning of Punjab in 1947. Welsh dissidents and mercenaries frequently fought for foreign powers, too, and Welsh pirates like Henry Morgan fought with any amount of *hwyl* on their own behalf.

Perhaps the most famous of all Welsh soldiers, Shakespeare's

LLYN TEGID, BALA, GWYNEDD   OCTOBER

MYNYDD PEN-Y-FAL, GWENT   JANUARY

MR & MRS HERBERT, CAPEL DEWI, DYFED   APRIL

TOM COWCHER, PEN-RHIW, CAPEL DEWI, DYFED   DECEMBER

Fluellen (an English misconception, by the way, of the name Llewelyn) was a somewhat pedantic scholar of the formal military arts. The traditional Welsh way of war, though, was the guerrilla way. Norman invasions of Wales were repeatedly frustrated by guerrilla tactics; in the fifteenth century the rebel Owain Glyndŵr and his Welshmen, by sudden forays out of the mountains, by night raids and fitful skirmishes, kept the forces of the Crown in a state of baffled confusion for months at a time. And the guerrilla instinct is alive in Wales to this day, among that sizeable minority of the Welsh people, most of them young and all ardent, who feel themselves oppressed still by the governance and even more perhaps the example of the English. Here is the fire of contemporary Wales in its most literal kind. Fire, they say, is the first weapon of the oppressed, and when these patriots turn to force they usually employ arson. In 1936 three respectable educationalists started the trend by setting fire to an air force installation in Llŷn: nowadays it is the smoke from a burning English-owned holiday home which, more often than not, proclaims the passing of the guerrillas.

The presence of the unappeasable patriots contributes powerfully to the elemental effects of Wales. They range from pacifist constitutional reformers to violent revolutionaries, and they provide a vivid extra streak to the texture of Welsh life, unpredictable and potentially dangerous. Rumours of subversion, tales of repression, run intermittently through the affairs of this little country, colouring its attitudes and its reputation and adding an undeniable extra *frisson* to its life. Telephones are tapped, secret policemen are unmasked, activists are jailed, houses are raided, militant

DEVIL'S BRIDGE, DYFED   NOVEMBER

CASTELL Y GWYNT, SNOWDONIA, GWYNEDD   JULY

LLYN CWM BYCHAN, RHINOGS, GWYNEDD   AUGUST

movements with threatening names briefly surface – the Free Wales Army, the Welsh Republican Movement, the Movement for Welsh Liberation, the Sons of Glyndŵr. Year after year the students demonstrate, slogan upon slogan is scrawled on bridge or court-house wall; and now and again the ancient discontent breaks into violence once more, a bomb goes off, an office is occupied, or more likely yet another holiday cottage is put to the torch, and its flickering flames high on the mountainside, the thin pillar of smoke that remains when dawn breaks, remind us once again that Wales is not an easy country, but burns always, in secret places of the landscape and unyielding recesses of the collective unconscious, with an inflexible and vindictive resentment.

AWYR : AIR

Air is the most Welsh element of all. There is a strangely suggestive quality to the vapour of this place. Some people never sense it, for the particular innuendoes of Wales, which so bewitch its confidants, altogether elude those who are out of sympathy: they see nothing but the skimble-skamble of the Welsh idiom, romantic fancy dressed up in hyperbole and shoved down their throats by unremitting essayists.

But then the idea of Welshness is essentially volatile and insubstantial – something in the air. When the Welsh poet Henry Vaughan envisaged heaven, he saw it as 'the world of light': but when he looked out upon his beloved Breconshire, it was in terms of lightness that he saw it too – not as meadows, not as mountains, but as a prospect intangible as the atmosphere itself. There is a Welsh art form which orchestrates these mystic instincts. It is called *canu penillion*, singing stanzas, and in it a poem written according to the strictest rules of Welsh prosody is sung to the accompaniment of the harp; but harper and singer perform different melodies, pursue different beats in a twangy floating discord until, as

LLYN PEN-FATHOR, BRECON BEACONS, POWYS   APRIL

theme and thought approach a conclusion, the chords gradually resolve themselves, the rhythms are synchronized, and the uneasy opposition is reconciled. It is hardly like a song at all: more like something on the wind, off the moor, or out of the world of light.

To its aficionados the air of Wales is like a drug. There is not much rationality to this obsession, and still less self-advantage, for the hope of Wales is certainly not the promise of universal glory: yet obsession it is. A well-known game among Welsh patriots is to see who can go longest without mentioning the name of Wales – a short contest generally, for so many strands of thought, so many allusions, lead every conversation inescapably back to the old addiction.

Like so much else in this ambiguous country, the air can be deceptive. The towns of the west Glamorgan industrial valleys, for example, hardly seem the sort of place where the music of *penillion* might be heard – congested, plain industrial towns, apparently wholly Anglicized, where you might suppose the values of bingo and the TV quiz game to be altogether supreme: in fact they are lively with Welsh tastes and traditions, resound with the Welsh language, and boast of bards on every corner. Even in parts where the language has been dead for generations and the last of the poets has packed away his harp for good, the idea of Welshness often gently lingers, and the distinctiveness of the country is still apparent. The administrative border that divides Wales from England runs very roughly along the line of Offa's Dyke, created by the Saxon King Offa in the eighth century to keep the two peoples apart, and it is still recognizably a frontier, a line between memories, and traditions, and sensibilities.

A village called Llanymynech, on the border between Welsh Powys and English Shropshire, piquantly illustrates the point. It looks just how you expect a small frontier town to look – a huddle of houses and inns around a road junction, overlooked on the Welsh side by a line of bluffs, on the English side surveying rich farms and flatlands. The pubs, one feels, might easily be clustered around a customs post. The garage looks as though it might offer favourable exchange rates. The shops seem to provide a last chance of buying Welsh cheese, wool or Locally Crafted Boot-Removers before you cross the line. With luck there might be a duty-free store.

And this fancy, as it happens, is almost ludicrously true, for not only is Llanymynech actually on Offa's Dyke, but the contemporary border between the two countries runs down the middle of its main street. Here one culture really does meet another in the middle of the traffic, and a thousand years of differing and often conflicting traditions face each other over the pavements. The line runs through the parish churchyard, behind the second tree from the road, and it bisects the Lion Hotel, whose landlord pays rates to both English and Welsh taxing authorities, and whose bar is divided jocularly down the middle by a frontier sign. They say there are people buried in Llanymynech half in one country, half in the other: their heads in Heaven, their feet in the other place.

Which is which is a matter of opinion, but most visitors, crossing that frontier, recognize some subtle shift of atmosphere (possibly because,

CARNMENYN, MYNYDD PRESCELLY, DYFED   JULY

BRAICH Y DDEUGWM, SNOWDONIA, GWYNEDD   JANUARY

while the signs on the English side merely announce it to be Shropshire, or Cheshire, the signs on the Welsh side cry *Croeso i Gymru!* – Welcome to Wales!). Along the border, where not much Welsh is spoken, this change of temperament is unlikely to be caused by a change of language, so Welshmen generally attribute it to an abstraction they hazily identify as 'The Welsh Way of Life'.

No doubt about it, this is something in the air. The very concept of a Welsh Way raises horse-laughs among Englishmen, to whom Welsh living habits often look like poor parodies of their own, but behind the superficial appearances there really is something distinctive, and powerful, to the Welsh social system. Its origins are clear enough: they lie in the general poverty of the country, in the deep traditional influence of religion, in the old love of music and poetry, in long centuries of conflict with the English, in the power of the Welsh language, in the ancient Celtic style of things, tribal in its loyalties, scattered in its locations. The general Anglicization of the gentry, starting in the fifteenth century, meant that the mass of the Welsh people, the *gwerin* or common folk, were not bound by the same ties of common interest that bound the English peasant to his squire: they found leaders of their own, mostly men of God or men of letters, and they were united in strong radical convictions that have made Wales into our own time a stronghold of the political Left.

Out of all this has developed an anomalous Welsh combination of individualism and commonality – The Welsh Way of Life. The individualism is illustrated splendidly by the long line of the Welsh eccentrics, of whom there has always been a plethora. I can think almost without trying

MOELYBLITHCWM, GWYNEDD   MARCH

CAPEL DEWI, DYFED   MARCH

of a dozen flamboyant examples, living and dead. There is Dr William Price of Llantrisant, for example, who in 1884 made cremation legal in Britain by burning the body of his infant son, Jesus Christ, on a mountain-top; who wore green clothes and a hat with a fox-tail hanging down behind, and who christened his daughter Countess of Glamorgan. There is Iolo Morgannwg the eighteenth-century poet-forger, whose published collections of ancient Welsh poems included many superb examples by himself, and who invented the pseudo-Druidical trappings of the National Eisteddfod, declaring them to be as old as the megaliths. There is Dic Aberdaron, a well-known scholar-tramp of Georgian times who is said to have learnt 35 languages and spent his whole life compiling a Welsh–Hebrew–Greek dictionary which was never to be published. There is R. J. Lloyd Price of Rhiwlas, who died in the 1920s after a life of glorious initiatives – the institution of sheep-dog trials, the production of Welsh whiskey, the authorship of *Dogs' Tales Wagged*, all overlaid by the spectacular ups and downs of sporting life. As it says on his tomb at Bala:

> *As To My Latter End I Go*
> *To Win My Jubilee,*
> *I Bless The Good Horse Bendigo*
> *Who Built This Tomb For Me.*

In almost every town and village of Wales you will find some more anonymous example: the reclusive student of seaweeds, the crank of the Feathers Inn, the woman up the valley who is known to cast spells, the doctor who habitually takes waders and fishing rods on house calls, the colourfully unsociable farmer, the preposterously ostentatious solicitor, the ever-heretical cleric.

As for the commonality, it is embodied especially in a particular kind of tight-knit brotherhood, together with cultural standards that have nothing to do with economic circumstance. By and large, even now, this is a more egalitarian society than most – certainly than England. In the Welsh-speaking, Calvinist country areas this still means the tightest kind of family cohesion, Jones by Jones, Evans by Evans, against all calumny or misfortune. In the industrial parts it has meant the cohesion of whole communities or callings: no towns were ever more united than the valley towns of the south, no craft or guild was ever more loyal to itself than the Welsh Miners' Federation. Welsh people wrenched from such comrade-ships often pine for them ever after, and residents of the grimmest coal valleys habitually swear that there is nowhere like Treorchy, not another Abertillery in the world.

If you want to feel, in the most tragic context, the collective identity of such a community, go to Aberfan, the village in Glamorganshire where, on 21 October 1966, 116 children and 26 adults were killed by a landslide from the coal tip above the town. A generation was lost at a stroke that day, and lies buried in one great graveyard on a hill above the town. Behind the graves the scrubby hillside rises towards the mountain ridge, below them the town clusters hugger-mugger around its pit-head in the valley. It is an emblematic site, so absolutely Welsh, so unmistakably of the valleys, and emblematic too in the long, long row of tombs, arranged in terraces

AFON ELAN, POWYS   OCTOBER

CAPEL DEWI, DYFED   DECEMBER

themselves like marble apotheoses of the houses far below, as though even in death they did not care to part from old patterns. Nowhere could be sadder, nowhere more proper to its meaning, and on a chill autumn Sunday, when there are still a few people tending to their children's graves or moving about with pots of flowers, it can seem as though the whole heart and hope of a people is buried up there on the hill.

As it happens many of those children had English names, their families having come to South Wales, no doubt, to find work in the heyday of the coalpits. They all died Welsh, though. Today one of the chief threats to the Welsh identity is the influx of English people, but in the past Wales has easily absorbed most of its invaders. Norman lords have been turned into Welsh landowners, Viking raiders have left behind their heritage of red hair and freckled noses, and the Flemings who settled in Gower and South Pembrokeshire, though they have never been in the least Welshized, long ago came to terms with their circumstances, and learnt to leave well alone. Even today garage men with rich Birmingham accents father children of purest Welshness, and some of the boldest Welsh patriots were born on the wrong side of Offa's Dyke.

For the Welsh air is full of old influences, more felt than understood. The tenacious genius of the place is more potent than it seems. The long line of Welsh poets, though they wrote in a language most Welshmen do not now understand, have left their strains and echoes in the public mind for ever, and even the most prosaic heart can hardly resist the spell of the ubiquitous Welsh legends, so full of surprise and beguilement. The

AFON TEIFI, TREGARON, DYFED   MAY

MAWDDACH ESTUARY & CADER IDRIS, GWYNEDD   MARCH

constancy of the place is all around: this is precisely the same soft air, one feels, that lay upon these landscapes in the days of the saints, the same winds blow off the sea, the rivers run through the same rocks, and even the same songs sound. The language itself, whether you speak it or not, whether you love it or hate it, is like some bewitchment or seduction from the past, drifting across the country down the centuries, subtly affecting the nation's sensibilities even when its meaning is forgotten.

All this is the air of Wales. No wonder the Welsh Way of Life, which is the air made human, can never be exactly defined or even easily recognized, still less institutionalized or built into monuments. Down in the Aberfan valley, at the spot where the tip came tumbling off the slope that day, the authorities have made a small memorial garden. The people do not seem to care much for it, though, and it is blown about by litter, and scrawled over with heedless graffiti.

So they seem to suggest themselves, the elements of Wales, as I stand at my window in the morning, or look at the pictures in this book. Is there a single image to be detected in them, as they form and blur and dissolve again? Only, I think, that metaphysical image of otherness – the secret separateness of the stone circles – the folk-tale delusions of time and space – the historical myths of Wales, their lost heroes wandering still from cavern to cavern in the hills – the half-hidden Welsh culture, with its unsuspected rhythms and unfamiliar forms – the illusory landscape of Wales itself, so grand a landscape for so small a country, built it seems for other proportions of achievement or aspiration, to another scale of history.

The presence of that other state of being constitutes a peculiar kind of unity. It is certainly not political unity, or linguistic, or even cultural. It is not physical unity either, for Gwynedd people are very different from the people of Dyfed, say, just as the mountains of Eryri, so wild and fierce, are a world away from the cosy farms and villages of Gower or the Glamorgan vale. It is the unity rather of the otherness itself, the idea of Welshness rather than the fact, expressing itself in the substance of the earth, the flow of the water, the heat of the fire, the opaque and moody screen of the air.

There are plenty of Welshmen who do not admit the compulsion of this unity, but as a hidden lodestone affects a compass, so I suspect its ancient presence affects most of them, despite themselves. And for those of us who have surrendered to it, to its misty fabric and its even mistier suggestion, it is like the pull of something so old, so grand, so strange that we cannot even envisage it, let alone put it into words, but instead respond to it instinctively, with a sense of wonder: as we all must, when we feel ourselves close to the beginning of things.

CERDDI : POEMS

MARWNAD OWAIN AB URIEN

Enaid Owain ab Urien,
    Gobwyllid Rheen o'i raid.
Rheged udd ae cudd tromlas,
    Nid oedd fas ei gywyddaid.
Isgell gŵr cerddglyd clodfawr,
    Esgyll gwawr gwaywawr llifaid,
Cany cheffir cystedlydd
    I udd Llwyfenydd llathraid,
Medel galon . . .

Gŵr gwiw uch ei amliw seirch
    A roddai feirch i eirchiaid.
Cyd as cronnai mal caled,
    Rhy ranned rhag ei enaid.
Enaid Owain ab Urien,
    Gobwyllid Rheen o'i raid.

TALIESIN (6th century)

ELEGY FOR OWAIN AB URIEN

The soul of Owain ab Urien,
May the Lord consider the need of him.
The heavy turf hides the lord of Rheged,
He was no shallow subject for praise.
A man renowned in song, greatly famed, beneath the ground.
His sharpened spears were like the wings of the dawn:
There is no rival
To the bright lord of Llwyfenydd,
Reaper of enemies . . .

A fine man in his many-coloured armour,
Who gave horses to supplicants,
Though he hoarded like a miser,
He gave for his soul's sake.
The soul of Owain ab Urien,
May the Lord consider the need of him.

trans. Twm Morys

WYE VALLEY, GWENT   JUNE

PAIS DINOGAD : HWIANGERDD

Pais Dinogad, fraith fraith,
O grwyn balaod ban wraith:
Chwid, chwid, chwidogaith,
Gochanwn, gochenyn' wythgaith.
Pan elai dy dad di i heliaw,
Llath ar ey ysgwydd, llory yn ei law,
Ef gelwi gŵn gogyhwg –
'Giff, gaff; daly, daly, dwg, dwg.'
Ef lleddi bysg yng nghorwg
Mal ban lladd llew llywiwg.
Pan elai dy dad dy i fynydd,
Dyddygai ef pen iwrch, pen gwythwch, pen hydd,
Pen grugiar fraith o fynydd,
Pen pysg o Raeadr Derwennydd.
O'r sawl yd gyrhaeddai dy dad di â'i gigwain
O wythwch a llewyn a llwynain
Nid angai oll ni fai oradain.

ANONYMOUS (7th century)

DINOGAD'S TUNIC : A LULLABY

Dinogad's tunic, speckled, speckled,
From weasel skins I made it:
Whoops, whoops a-whistle
We'll sing, and the eight bondsmen will sing.
When your father went hunting,
A spear on his shoulder and a club in his hand,
He'd call the fast dogs —
'Giff, Gaff! Catch, catch, fetch, fetch!'
He'd strike fish in his coracle
As a lion strikes the llywiwg.
When your father went to the mountain
He'd bring a buck, a boar, a stag,
A grouse from the mountain,
A fish from Derwennydd Falls.
Of all the boars, foxes and beasts of the wood
That your father reached with his spear
None escaped, unless it was winged!

trans. Twm Morys

BRAICH Y DDEUGWM, SNOWDONIA, GWYNEDD   JANUARY

MARWNAD
LLYWELYN AP GRUFFUDD

Poni welwch-chwi hynt y gwynt a'r glaw?
Poni welwch-chwi'r deri'n ymdaraw?
Poni welwch-chwi'r môr yn merwinaw – 'r tir?
Poni welwch-chwi'r gwir yn ymgweiriaw?
Poni welwch-chwi'r haul yn hwylaw – 'r awyr?
Poni welwch-chwi'r sŷr wedi r'syrthiaw?
Poni chredwch-chwi i Dduw, ddyniadon ynfyd?
Poni welwch-chwi'r byd wedi r'bydiaw?
Och hyd atat-ti, Dduw, na ddaw – môr dros dir!
Pa beth y'n gedir i ohiriaw?
Nid oes le y cyrcher rhag carchar braw;
Nid oes le y triger; och o'r trigaw!
    *   *   *

Gwae fi am arglwydd, gwalch diwaradwydd;
Gwae fi o'r aflwydd ei dramgwyddaw.
Gwae fi o'r golled, gwae fi o'r dynged,
Gwae fi o'r clywed fod clwyf arnaw.

GRUFFUDD AB YR YNAD COCH (fl. c. 1280)

ELEGY FOR LLYWELYN AP GRUFFUDD

Do you not see the path of the wind and the rain?
Do you not see the oaks beating together?
Do you not see the sea scouring the land?
Do you not see the truth fulfilling itself?
Do you not see the sun sailing the heavens?
Do you not see the stars fallen?
Do you not believe in God, simple men,
Do you not believe the world has ended?
Oh God! that the sea would not come over the land!
Why are we kept lingering?
There is no place to go from terror's grasp;
There is no place to stay; wretched is staying.
     *   *   *

Alas for my lord, blameless hawk.
Alas for the transgression he has suffered.
Alas for the loss, alas for the fate,
Alas for hearing there is a wound upon him.

trans. Twm Morys

YR WYLAN

Yr wylan deg ar lanw dioer
Unlliw ag eiry neu wenlloer,
Dilwch yn dy degwch di,
Darn fel haul, dyrnfol heli.
Ysgafn ar don eigion wyd,
Esgudfalch edn bysgodfwyd.
Yngo'r aud wrth yr angor
Lawlaw â mi, lili môr.
Llythr unwaith, llathr ei annwyd,
Lleian ym mrig llanw môr wyd.

Cyweirglod bun, câi'r glod bell,
Cyrch ystum caer a chastell.
Edrych a welych, wylan,
Eigr o liw ar y gaer lân.
Dywed fy ngeiriau duun.
Dewised fi, dos at fun.
Byddai'i hun, beiddia'i hannerch,
Bydd fedrus wrth foethus ferch
Er budd; dywed na byddaf,
Fwynwas coeth, fyw onis caf.

Ei charu'r wyf, gwbl nwyf nawdd —
Och wŷr! erioed ni charawdd
Na Myrddin wenieithfin iach,
Na Thaliesin ei thlysach.
Siprys dyn giprys dan gopr,
Rhagorbryd, rhy gyweirbropr!
Och wylan, o chai weled
Grudd y ddyn lanaf o Gred,
Oni chaf fwynaf annerch
Fy nihenydd fydd y ferch.

DAFYDD AP GWILYM (fl. 1340-70)

THE SEAGULL

The fair seagull on the tide,
The very same colour as snow or moonlight,
Your fairness is spotless,
A scrap like the sun, glove of the sea,
You are light upon the ocean wave,
Swift, proud fish-eating bird!
Go there by the anchor,
Hand in hand with me, sea-lily.
Like a bright-looking letter,
You are a nun upon the sea-tide.

Girl's praise, she'll have far praise —
Go to the bend of wall and castle,
Look if you can see, seagull,
That Eigr on the bright wall.
Say my acceptable words.
May she choose me! Go to the girl.
If she's alone, be bold to greet her,
Be clever with the delicate girl,
To win her. Say I'll not
Live, a gentle fellow, unless I have her.

I love her, cause of all passion.
Oh men! Never did smooth-mouthed Merlin
Or Taliesin love one more lovely than her,
Cypress-like, fought for, under copper hair,
Most beautiful, too proper!
Oh seagull, if you see
The cheek of the loveliest girl in Christendom,
Unless I have the sweetest of greetings,
The girl will be my end.

trans. Twm Morys

CLOCAENOG FOREST, CLWYD   APRIL

CYNGOR Y LLWYNOG

'Dydd da i'r llwynog o'r ogof,
Gelyn pob aderyn dof,
Dy waneg a adwaenwn,
Croeso'n wir i'r rhwydd-dir hwn . . .
Dysg im yn rhodd fodd i fwy;
Pe rhoit gyngor rhagorawl,
Gwnaud fyth im ganu dy fawl.'

      *   *   *

'Nid hawdd heddyw byw heb wad,
Er a geir o wir gariad.
O mynni fyw yma'n faith,
Dos ag enw, dysg weniaith,
Ac ar weniaith pob gronyn,
Dysg fedru bradychu dyn.
Dywed yn deg am neges,
O'th law na ollwng mo'th les;
Dywed bob geiriau duwiol,
A'th drais a'th falais i'th fol.
Nad i un wedi'i eni
Wybod mewn man d'amcan di.
Dyna'r ffordd'r adwaenir ffwl,
Fo a addef ei feddwl.
Treisio'r gwan nid traws yw'r gwaith,
Trinia gadarn trwy weniaith.
Gwna bob drwg heb ei ddiw'giaw,
Iti, ddyn, byd da a ddaw.

      *   *   *

Ci a welaf yn calyn,
Nid hawdd im siarad ond hyn,
Nac aros ym min gorallt;
Ffarwel, rhaid im ffoi i'r allt.'

HUW LLWYD (c. 1568-c. 1630)

THE FOX'S ADVICE

'Good day to the fox of the cave,
Enemy of every tame bird,
I recognize your shape.
Welcome to this generous land . . .
Teach me as a gift the way to live;
If you give me good advice
I'll sing your praise for ever.'

      *   *   *

It's not easy to live today, no denying,
Despite what there is of true love.
If you wish to live here long,
Forget reputation, learn flattery,
And every subtlety of flattery,
Learn how to deceive men.
Talk sweetly of your errand,
Do not let your profit fall from your hand.
Say all holy words,
With your violence and your malice in your belly.
Do not let a soul born
Know your purpose anywhere.
That's the way a fool is known,
He admits his thoughts.
Oppress the weak, that's the way,
And deal with the strong by flattery.
Do every wrong without righting it,
And to you, man, good fortune will come.

      *   *   *

I see a dog following,
It's not easy for me to say more,
Or stay at the foot of the hill;
Farewell, I must flee to the hillside.'

trans. Twm Morys

GLYDER FACH, SNOWDONIA, GWYNEDD   JANUARY

CARIAD AT DDUW

'Rwy'n edrych dros y bryniau pell
   Amdanat bob yr awr;
Tyrd, fy Anwylyd, mae'n hwyrhau
   A'm haul bron mynd i lawr.

Trôdd fy nghariadau oll i gyd
   'Nawr yn anffyddlon im;
Ond yr wyf finnau'n hyfryd glaf
   O gariad mwy ei rym.

*   *   *

'Does gyflwr tan yr awyr las
   'Rwy'ynddo'n chwennych byw;
Ond fy hyfrydwch fyth gaiff fod
   O fewn cynteddau'm Duw.

Fe ddarfu blas, fe ddarfu chwant
   At holl bwysiau'r byd;
Nid oes ond gwagedd heb ddim trai
   Yn rheged trwyddo i gyd.

WILLIAM WILLIAMS, PANTYCELIN (1717-91)

LOVE FOR GOD

Over the distant hills I gaze
  Expectant for thee yet;
O come, my Dear, the hour is late,
  My sun is almost set.

Failed my old loves, every one,
  To keep their faith for long;
But sweetly heart-sick I embrace
  A love for ever strong.
   *   *   *
I do not yearn for consequence
  Beneath an earthly light;
Only the hospitality of God
  Can give me my delight.

The taste has gone, the lust has gone,
  For this world's rise and fall;
Only a tide of vanity
  Flows ebbless through it all.

trans. Jan Morris

AFON YSTWYTH, CAMBRIAN MOUNTAINS, DYFED   OCTOBER

LLYS IFOR HAEL

Llys Ifor Hael, gwael yw'r gwedd, –yn garnau
    Mewn gwerni mae'n gorwedd;
    Drain ac ysgall mall a'i medd,
    Mieri lle bu mawredd.

Yno nid oes awenydd, –na beirddion,
    Na byrddau llawenydd,
    Nac aur yn ei magwyrydd,
    Na mael, na gŵr hael a'i rhydd.

I Ddafydd gelfydd ey gân–oer ofid
    Roi Ifor mewn graean;
    Mwy echrys fod ei lys lân
    Yn lleoedd i'r dylluan.

Er bri arglwyddi byr glod, –eu mawredd
    A'u muriau sy'n darfod;
    Lle rhyfedd i falchedd fod
    Yw teiau ar y tywod.

EVAN EVANS, IEUAN FARDD (1731-88)

THE HALL OF IFOR HAEL

Ifor Hael's hall, how wretched it looks
　　　　Lying in heaps in marshes;
　　　Thorns and accursed thistles own it,
　　　Briars where greatness has been.

There is no inspiration there,
　　　　No poets, no tables of merriment,
　　　No gold inside its walls,
　　　No bounty, no generous man to give it.

A cold grief for Dafydd, of the skilled song,
　　　　Putting Ifor in the earth;
　　　More terrible that his fair courts
　　　Are the owl's places.

For all the glory of short-famed lords
　　　　Their splendour and their walls come to an end:
　　　A strange place for pride to be–
　　　Houses in the sand.

trans. Twm Morys

YR HENIAITH

Disglair yw eu coronau yn llewych llysoedd
A thanynt hwythau. Ond nid harddach na hon
Sydd yn crwydro gan ymwrando â lleisiau
Ar ddisberod o'i gwrogaeth hen;
Ac sydd yn holi pa yfory a fydd,
Holi yng nghyrn y gorllewinwynt heno—
Udo gyddfau'r tyllau a'r ogofáu
Dros y rhai sy'n annheilwing o hon.

Ni sylwem arni. Hi oedd y goleuni, heb liw.
Ni sylwem arni, yr awyr a ddaliai'r arogl
I'n ffroenau. Dwfr ein genau, goleuni blas.
Ni chlywem ei breichiau am ei bro ddi-berygl
Ond mae tir ni ddring ehedydd yn ôl i'w nen,
Rhyw ddoe dihiraeth a'u gwahanodd.
Hyn yw gaeaf cenedl, y galon oer
Heb wybod colli ei phum llawenydd.

Na! dychwel gwanwyn i un a noddai
Ddeffrowyr cenhedloedd cyn eu haf.
Hael y tywalltai ei gwin iddynt.
Codent o'i byrddau dros bob hardd yn hyf.
Nyni, a wêl ei hurddas trwy niwl ei hadfyd,
Codwn yma yr hen feini annistryw.
Pwy yw'r rhain trwy'r cwmwl a'r haul yn hedfan,
Yn dyfod fel colomennod i'w ffenestri?

WALDO WILLIAMS (1904-71)

THE OLD LANGUAGE

Bright are their crowns in the lustre of courts
And under them. But not fairer than she
Who wanders listening to the voices
Scattered from her ancient homage,
And who asks what tomorrow there will be,
Asking in the horns of the west wind tonight,
The howling of the holes and the caves,
For those unworthy of her.

We did not notice her. She was the light without colour.
We did not notice her, the air which carried the scent
To our nostrils. The water of our mouth, the light of taste.
We did not feel her arms about her unendangered country.
But there is a land where the lark will not climb back into its heaven,
Some yesterday without hiraeth has estranged them.
This is the winter of a nation, the cold heart
Unconscious of the loss of its five delights.

No! Spring will return to one who fostered
The wakers of nations before their summer.
Liberally it poured her wine for them.
And they rose boldly from her tables for all things beautiful.
And we, who see her dignity through the mist of her misfortune,
Let us lift, here, the old undestroyed stones.
Who are these through the cloud and the sun flying,
Coming like doves to her windows?

trans. Twm Morys

ABOVE BRISTLY RIDGE, SNOWDONIA, GWYNEDD   MAY

TRI HYNAIF BYD

Tyllvan Gwm Kowlwyd,
Eryr Gwern Abwy,
A Mwyalchen Gelli Gadarn.

THREE ELDERS OF THE WORLD

Owl of Cwm Cowlwyd,
Eagle of Gwernabwy,
Blackbird of Celli Gadarn.